EYES THAT SEE

EYES THAT SEE

BASED ON A PROPHETIC VISION
THROUGH

PATRICIA KING

Published by XP Publishing
A department of Christian Services Association
P.O. Box 1017, Maricopa, Arizona 85139
www.XPpublishing.com

ISBN-13: 978-1-936101-26-9
ISBN-10: 1-936101-26-2

Printed in Canada. For worldwide distribution.

Dedicated to

All my "Seer Friends"
who have taught me so much
about the seer dimension.

TABLE OF CONTENTS

FOREWORD
BY ROBERT HOTCHKIN

When Jesus walked the earth as a man, He was here to share the reality of the Kingdom with all who were willing to receive it. In every situation He encountered, He knew what to do because He had eyes to see (John 5:19).

We are the Body of Christ in the earth today. Because Jesus came as a man and fulfilled our part of the covenant by living perfectly and shedding His blood on our behalf, we have been restored to the fullness of relationship with our Heavenly Father. We now are His children in the earth, and we too are here to show those around us the reality of the Kingdom. Just as when Jesus, the firstborn of many sons (Romans 8:29), was here on earth, the Father wants to show you, His precious child, what He is doing so that you can cooperate with Him. You are called to do the works that Jesus did (John 14:12). Everything that Jesus did began with seeing what His Father was doing; it began by seeing into the Divine Realm and then loosing that into the earth. It began with eyes that see.

When we read Revelation 4, we see that there are citizens of heaven covered with eyes so that they may behold the Lord. You, being born-again, are also now a citizen of heaven, and the Lord longs for you to behold Him and His glory. He has given you eyes, and His desire is that you allow Him to open them so that you might see (Revelation 3:18).

You wouldn't be holding this book if your heart didn't echo the Lord's cry that your eyes be opened. Something in you already knows you were made to see Him, and gaze upon Him, and behold Him, and be filled with Him more intimately and fully than ever before. Something in you is longing to see what He is doing in the earth right now, so that you can participate in it and give Him glory.

Even after all the Apostle Paul had seen and known of Jesus, that wasn't enough. He knew there was more and he cried out for it, declaring that his only desire was to know the Lord, His Kingdom, His power, and His ways, to an even greater degree (Philippians 3:10-11). The Lord answered that cry by opening Paul's eyes to look forward, to look at the prize of the upward call in Christ Jesus. And the Lord will answer your "More, Lord!" cry, as well.

Perhaps that prayer of yours for more of Him - to behold, gaze upon, and see Him more - is a part of why He stirred Patricia King to write this book. In the revelation that she shares in EYES THAT SEE, she comes alongside of you much as Elisha came alongside of the young man in 2 Kings 2:17. Elisha prayed that the Lord would open the eyes of that young man so that he could see into the heavenlies and be aware of the activities of the Kingdom in the earth. In EYES THAT SEE, Patricia helps lead you into that same place of open-eyed beholding and wonder.

In this book, Patricia unpacks Scripture to help give you biblical understanding of what the Lord has made available to you – how He has given you eyes to see in the spirit realm. She also outlines easy and practical ways for you to step into the seer gifting and begin seeing more of Him and His Kingdom, what He is doing in the earth, and how He sees you and those around you.

There is so much He wants to show you!

As you begin to activate your EYES THAT SEE, let me pray for you similarly to what Paul prayed for believers in his day:

Father God, I ask in the mighty name of our Lord Jesus, that You would give the precious ones who read this book the spirit of wisdom and revelation in the knowledge of Christ, and may the eyes You have given them to see in the Spirit be opened so that they will know You, Your ways, and all that You have made available to them through Your Son in a greater dimension than ever before. Amen.

Robert Hotchkin
Christian Services Association / XP

YOUR EYES

By *Patricia King*

Jesus,

Your eyes—
    Full of fire,
        Righteous flames...
            exposing, sifting, analyzing.
    Full of fire,
        Burning embers...
            melting, molding, transforming.

Jesus,
Your eyes—
    Full of longing,
        Searching for...
            hearts perfected, yielded, devoted.
    Full of longing,
        Revealing...
            passion, strength, might.

Jesus,
Your eyes—
    Full of wisdom,
        Illuminating...
            counsel, guidance, understanding.
    Full of wisdom,
        Revealing...
            truth, secrets, mysteries.

Jesus,
    Your eyes—
        Love.

Two Spiritual Visions

Dear Reader,

It is my desire that, through reading this book, your spiritual sight will be awakened and you will explore new dimensions of the Lord's glory and truth. In January 2003, I received the following visions.

The Vision of the Eyes

During a time of meditation, prayer, and study, I saw a spiritual vision of the throne room in heaven, with eyes everywhere. The backdrop of the vision was made up of shimmering, pulsating, and illuminating emerald-green light. I saw nothing except the emerald green backdrop, the eyes, and a throne made of fiery flames. I saw no human form, only the flames of His throne and His fiery presence. The eyes varied in size, appearance, and color, but they were all beholding the Lord on His throne.

The Lord revealed that He was about to release increased visionary perception of His presence and glory as His people spend time in "throne-room worship." Revelation 1, 4, and 5; Ezekiel 1; Daniel 7:9-14; and Isaiah 6:1-8 are key passages to this vision as the Lord gives His people invitation in this *Kairos* (God-appointed time). The Holy Spirit is going to bring forth a great increase of revelation in the knowledge of Christ as believers seek to know Him. The spiritual eyes of believers will be opened in these coming days to more of the glory, reality, wisdom, majesty, and strategies of the Kingdom.

THE VISION OF THE EYE SALVE

I saw a vision of a golden bowl in the heavenly places with the words "eye salve" engraved on it. Believers were approaching the bowl and anointing their eyes with the salve. The salve had a profound effect on those who received it—their vision opened to behold the glory and the deep things of the Kingdom. Hebrews 4:16 as well as Revelation 3:18 were highlighted during the vision: *"Come boldly to the throne of grace"* and *"anoint your eyes with eye salve, that you might see."*

The "salve" represents the sight of Jesus. The Body of Christ is standing at a threshold of increased spiritual revelation and will see the unfolding of many things that have been concealed by the Lord until this hour. Both young and old have opportunity to grow in visionary revelation and gifting at this time. The Holy Spirit will anoint those who hunger for "heaven's eyes." Luke 4:18 was quickened to me during this visionary experience: "The Spirit of the LORD is upon Me...to proclaim liberty to the captives and *recovery of sight to the blind.*"

MY DESIRE FOR YOU

It is my desire that you will be supernaturally released into an increased revelatory dimension following the reading of this book. Your spiritual sight is able to behold many things: Jesus Himself through your personal devotion; His plans and strategies for the times we are living in; your potential in Christ; the Kingdom realm with all of Christ's glory within, as well as profound prophetic insights. May you experience keener perception and Kingdom insight as the Holy Spirit opens *"the eyes of your understanding"* (Ephesians 1:18). The awakening of your spiritual vision is one of the benefits of being His child. Blessings dear one— *God loves you with an everlasting love!*

Patricia King

CHAPTER 1

EYES THAT SEE

Therefore I also, after I heard of your faith in the Lord Jesus and your love for all saints, do not cease to give thanks for you, making mention of you in my prayers: that the God of our Lord Jesus Christ, the Father of glory, may give you the spirit of wisdom and revelation in the knowledge of Him, *the eyes* of your understanding being enlightened; that you may know what is the hope of His calling, what are the riches of the glory of His inheritance in the saints, and what is the exceeding greatness of His power toward us who believe, according to the working of His mighty power (Ephesians 1:15-19 NKJV, emphasis added).

The Apostle Paul prayed this prayer for the church at Ephesus because he knew the importance of seeing into the realm of the Kingdom. His desire was for them to *see* and know Christ, the greatness of His power towards believers, and their value to Him. This same prayer is the Lord's desire for you, too.

John the Beloved was the one who saw into the heavenly dimension. In the book of Revelation, John reveals what the throne room is like and portrays some glorious activity. For example, he describes four living creatures that are *"full of eyes around and within"* (Revelation 4:8b). That is a lot of eyes! These angelic beings constantly behold the Lamb and declare holy worship along with the other angels and elders that are stationed around the throne.

Even as these creatures have been given eyes to see, so have you. You are able to see into the Kingdom realm. It is simply a matter of having your spiritual sight enlightened by the Spirit of God. You, as one of God's children, have the ability to see (perceive) with spiritual vision the glory of Jesus through your eyes of faith. As you behold Him in magnificence, you will, along with the host of heaven, also fall down and worship Him who is worthy.

EYES THAT BEHOLD HIM

In Exodus 33:18, Moses said to the Lord, *"Please, show me Your glory."* The Lord said He would allow all of His goodness to pass before him and that He would proclaim the name of the Lord before him (see verse 19). The word *goodness* here is written in superlative tense. In other words,

God was explaining to Moses that He was going to reveal to him the maximum, superlative level of His goodness and that He would proclaim to Moses His very name. Moses was actually being promised the revelation of Christ. He was going to *see* the "goodness of the Father" and the "glory of the Father" in the face of Jesus Christ, as well as to understand the revelation of His name.

God further explained to Moses that, *"You cannot see My face; for no man shall see Me, and live"* (verse 20). The word *face* in this passage is in reference to the plural faces of God. In other words, God might have been saying to Moses, "No man, with human eyes and perspective, will be able to see the fullness of all that I am—I am just too *much* to take in." We can, however, see Him in the face and person of Jesus Christ. Jesus said in the New Testament, *"He who has seen Me has seen the Father"* (John 14:9). The writer of Hebrews further declares that Jesus is the exact representation of the Father and that the fullness of the Godhead dwells within Christ in bodily form (see Hebrews 1:3).

When we behold Him, we will be like Him. 2 Corinthians 3:18 states, "But we all with unveiled face, **beholding** as in a mirror the glory of the Lord, are being **transformed into the same image** from glory to glory, just as by the Spirit of the Lord" (emphasis added). This amazing power of transformation makes "beholding" extremely important.

LEARNING TO FOCUS

Many things in our daily life can distract us, causing us to behold and focus on natural circumstances rather than the Lord. The story of Mary and Martha describes this well. In Luke 10:38-42, we find Mary sitting at Jesus' feet undistracted while listening to His word. She was beholding Him. He was the very focus of her attention—He was all she could *see*—everything else appeared dim and insignificant in the light of His presence. Martha, on the other hand, *"was distracted with all her preparations"* (NASB). Her vision was fixed on all the natural tasks at hand and she therefore failed to see the glory and the value of the One in their midst.

In John 12:1-9, we find Mary taking a pound of very costly perfume of pure nard and anointing the feet of Jesus. Perhaps, during the time recorded in Luke 10 that she spent sitting at His feet, she had received teaching and revelation concerning Christ's journey to the cross. As a result, she was able to truly understand the depth of what she was called to do as she anointed Him for burial. Judas, and possibly others in the room, did not understand what she was doing. This depth of revelation and faith can only be birthed in His presence.

Mary chose a posture that enabled her to behold. She turned away from the distractions around her and took time to visit with Jesus, listening to His teachings. This is a key for us, also. There will always be tasks at hand, and life will always seem to have its pressures. Jesus explained to Martha in the midst of her anxiety that there was really only one important thing and that Mary had chosen it. He was attempting to show her that *sitting* in his presence is better than *serving* in His presence. Both are important, of course, and I am not endorsing laziness, but we need to have first things first.

If we, like Mary, will take time to focus on Jesus, His Word, and His beauty, then we will also be choosing the better part. Jesus is always to be the central focus of our lives. May the eyes of our hearts constantly be drawn to gaze upon His loveliness.

BEHOLDING PRODUCES A WORSHIPPING HEART

When we spend time beholding the Lord, our heart rises up to respond to the awesomeness of His being. In Revelation 4:8, we find the four living creatures in the presence of the Lord, with eyes around and within. We know for sure that they were beholding; that is what you do with eyes—you look, gaze, behold. The response to their beholding was non-stop, continuous worship. *"And they do not rest day or night, saying: 'Holy, holy, holy, Lord God Almighty, Who was and is and is to come!'"*

In the same chapter, we find that there were 24 elders around the throne in the Lord's presence, beholding Him.

In verses 10 and 11, we find that they also responded with worship, throwing their crowns before Him and declaring His worth with intense passion.

This response will be ours, also, as we spend time focused on Him. He is worthy to be worshipped, and worship is spontaneous when you gaze into His likeness.

PREPARATION FOR BEHOLDING

The following are some helpful, practical tips that will prepare you to behold Him in your devotional time:

1. **Set a time for seeking Him each day.** Mark it in your daily appointment calendar. It is advisable to set aside about an hour a day. This will give you time to focus. If you have a busy schedule, you might need to rise up earlier or go to bed later. Make this special time a priority. Find a time of day when you have the least amount of distractions and demands.

2. **Find a comfortable, quiet place.** Is there a special room in your home where you can meet with Him? I have known some people to have a prayer closet—a literal closet. During an experience on the mission field a number of years ago, I stayed in a dormitory with eleven other women for one week. The place was very crowded. We were in the inner city of a large metropolis and there seemed to be no options

outdoors, either, for time alone with God. I found absolutely no place in that environment to escape to. Necessity is the mother of invention, so I climbed into my bunk and pulled the covers over my head. I informed everyone that this was my quiet place with the Lord and I was not to be disturbed when under the sheet. It worked! We just have to do what we have to do.

3. **Focus on Jesus.** Begin to turn your attention towards Him; tell Him how much you love Him; think on His goodness. If you find your mind being distracted, pull your thoughts back into focus. Most often, *beholding* is simply found in the quiet meditation of the heart.

4. **Read some Scripture** and invite the Lord to reveal Himself to you through the Word you are meditating on. Sometimes, I like to meditate on the portions of Scripture that describe Jesus' appearance, such as the verses you find in Revelation 1. This is beholding, not with an open vision, but with the vision of the Scripture.

5. **Pray.** Ask Jesus to reveal His heart to you. Invite Him to lead you into discovery of His fullness.

6. **Journal any insights you receive from Him** during your time with Him. Meditate on these things

throughout the day. Think about what Jesus is like through the things He has revealed.

7. **Take time throughout the day** to turn your focus towards Him.

PRAYER FOR EYES THAT BEHOLD

Father, I invite You to open the eyes of my heart and grant me a spirit of wisdom and revelation in the knowledge of Jesus Christ. Open my eyes to behold Your glory and the glory of Your Kingdom. May I have a heart like Mary, who sits and beholds You, receiving Your Word and wisdom. May I be like the living creatures and the elders around the throne, who worship You with such clarity and holy response. May I have eyes that see. Amen

CHAPTER 2

EYES THAT DISCERN THE TIMES

The Lord is always leading us from "glory to glory" (2 Corinthians 3:18) There are things that He desires to unfold to each generation, and there are seasons in the Kingdom that need to be discerned. As a young Christian I often prayed, "Lord, I always want to be right where You are. I don't want to run ahead of You or find myself too far behind You—I want to run *with* You."

I found that there are times and seasons for the Lord to unfold revelation and events to the Body. As I waited on Him, I would get a sense of what He was doing and saying in each new season. He always gave strategy and insight, and as a result, we have been privileged over the years to always follow the cloud!

THE SONS OF ISSACHAR

The sons of Issachar were a tribe in Israel who were specially gifted and called to discern the times. Using their discernment, they instructed Israel on how to respond to each new season in the Lord (see 1 Chronicles 12:32). We, as God's people, can have this type of sensitivity, vision, and wisdom today.

Take a look at the special hour we are living in. There are threats of terrorism, violence, and war. It is even feared that a nuclear holocaust might be close at hand. We see that moral decline and lawlessness have increased. The masses are generally feeling powerless in all the shakings around them. Education, family, career, material security, sexual fulfillment, and escapism through the drug scene have all fallen short in satisfying the deep inner needs in most hearts. As a result, we are seeing a growing emergence of spiritual hunger and awakening. The crowds are looking for answers and they are hungry for a spiritual awakening. Consequently, we have now entered an era of transition.

SIGNS ARE EVERYWHERE

Signs of this transition are everywhere. Many books and movies have a spiritual theme. The music industry is promoting "sounds of the spirit world." New Age practices have infiltrated the education system, the medical profession, the political realm, and the business world. Spiritual superheroes are being introduced through various means, drawing affections and imaginations towards "deliverers" who promise release and relief. Children's programs, cartoons, and games are often supernatural in nature. Satanic, occult, and New Age groups are growing dramatically as they continue to introduce hungry, new "converts" to the spirit world. Where is the Church in the midst of this counterfeit uprising? Are we discerning the transition? Are we operating in the wisdom and direction of God for this day?

WE CAN MAKE A DIFFERENCE

It is imperative at this critical time that we dedicate ourselves afresh to seeking the face of the Lord, receiving "eyes" that discern the times. Even though there are many discouraging things, there is also a plan - right from the heart of God - waiting to be unfolded to us. These are exciting times—perhaps the most exciting times in all of Church history. We need eyes to discern the will of God. We need to see Him and his power in the midst of these days.

In John 16:12-13, Jesus said to His disciples,

"I have many more things to say to you, but you cannot bear them now. But when He, the Spirit of truth comes, He will guide you into all the truth; for He will not speak on *His own initiative, but whatever He hears, He will speak; and He will disclose to you what is to come.*"

The Holy Spirit will give us discerning eyes, as well as wisdom and counsel for the current hour.

The way we did things before will not necessarily work today. A new wineskin is needed for this hour—but what will it look like? As we seek the Lord for wisdom, asking Him for eyes that see, we will then, like the sons of Issachar, discern the times and know what we must do.

PREPARATION FOR DISCERNING THE TIMES

The following are some helpful, practical tips that will prepare you to discern the times:

1. **Invite the Lord to give you a gift of discernment** that you might see His purposes in each season.

2. **Observe outward things**, like current local and world events, and obtain the general sense of what is happening in the world around you.

3. **Ask the Lord to reveal His special purposes and plans** for this hour. Write these things down and ponder them.

4. **Pray for the Lord to reveal to you how you are to live** in this hour. Ask Him to show you what you are to do.

5. **Begin to pray** into what the Lord reveals.

PRAYER FOR EYES THAT DISCERN

Father, I humbly ask that You give me eyes to discern Your presence, Your plans, and Your ways. I desire my spiritual perception to be like that which you gave the sons of Issachar. I desire to discern the times and to know how to walk with You that Your glory might fill the earth. Fulfill my desire, I pray. Amen

CHAPTER 3

EYES THAT SEE POTENTIAL

When we receive Christ as our Savior, we enter into an eternal covenant with God and are forever secure in His love. Everything that pertains to life and godliness has been given to us in this covenant, and every spiritual blessing in the heavenly places belongs to us (2 Peter 1:3; Ephesians 1:3). It is the Lord's desire that we enjoy the full, abundant life that He has promised to everyone who comes to Him (John 10:10).

Faith is the spiritual substance that connects us to these blessings. In order to believe, we need to receive revelation (insight) from the Lord.

In Genesis 13:14-15, we find the Lord speaking to Abraham. He said:

Lift your **eyes** now and look from the place where you are—northward, *southward, eastward, and westward;*

33

for all the land which you **see** *I give to you and your descendants forever (emphasis added).*

In other words, the Lord was saying to Abraham, "If you see it, you can have it."

What is the Lord showing you? The Lord revealed to Abraham his potential blessing in this particular situation. This revelation then produced faith in Abraham's heart, and he was therefore able to act on what he saw.

GIDEON THE MIGHTY WARRIOR

Gideon was a man who couldn't see his potential. In Judges 6:12, we find that the Lord sent His angel to Gideon to proclaim the true vision of who he was in God's sight. The angel said, *"The Lord is with you, you mighty man of valor!"* Gideon could not accept this word from the Lord because he perceived himself differently than what was declared over him. In verse 15, he responded, *"Indeed my clan is the weakest in Manasseh, and I am the least in my father's house."* He had a poor self-image, but the angel came with the revelation of the Lord's vision that had the potential to shatter the false image. All Gideon had to do was believe the true vision. Eventually, he was able to *see*, and as a result, he brought a great deliverance to his nation. Many believers fall short of their potential because they do not *see* all that the Lord has for them.

THE GOOD REPORT OF JOSHUA AND CALEB

Numbers 13 records God's directions to Moses to "spy out the land of Canaan, which I am going to give the sons of Israel." So Moses sent 12 men into the Promised Land to see what it was like. They all came back acknowledging the incredible potential the land had. Ten of the spies, however, chose to focus on the size of the cities, the strength of the people, and their potential loss to the giants in the land. Joshua and Caleb were the only ones who saw the true potential to defeat the inhabitants of the land with God's power. Unfortunately, Israel chose to side with the bad report and it was only Joshua and Caleb who were able to enter the Promised Land 40 years later because of their unique perspective (see Joshua 14:8-9).

DAVID THE GIANT KILLER

The story of David and Goliath is another example of how often it's just the few who see potential while the majority do not (1 Samuel 17). The army of Israel under Saul's rule was being taunted by a giant named Goliath. They could not see the victory. They saw through eyes of intimidation and not through eyes of faith. David, on the other hand, saw through covenant eyes. He knew that God would give him the victory—David saw his own potential. In faith, he pursued the giant and slew him. What a victory for Israel that day! David saw the potential victory in the midst of the adverse situation and went for it.

35

PETER THE ROCK

Jesus, in His earthly ministry, was always speaking potential over people's lives. He spoke encouraging and life-giving words over his disciples, the sick, the lepers, and even the dead. Jesus saw potential in his disciples. At the time He called them to follow Him, they looked like ordinary people with flaws in their characters and lives. He saw beyond their weaknesses and looked to their potential.

Peter is a great example of that, isn't he? Jesus called him a *rock* (John 1:42), when in the natural, Peter acted like a wimp. Jesus both saw and proclaimed Peter's potential, and as a result, Peter fulfilled his destiny.

YOU HAVE UNLOCKED POTENTIAL

You too have all kinds of potential that is yet to be unlocked. Invite Jesus to give you eyes to see this glorious potential. Ask Him to show you some covenant promises from His Word that you can respond to in faith—and then—believe!

PREPARATION TO SEE POTENTIAL

The following are some helpful, practical tips that will prepare you to see potential:

1. **Spend time around others who bring out the best in you** and encourage you to pursue God's best for your life. This will help you to see the potential in

yourself and develop strong, supportive relationships that help you grow in the Lord.

2. **Share with others the potential you see in them.** Do this often! Declare over them the truth of who God has created them to be. This can be something as simple as expressing your appreciation for a quality they consistently demonstrate.

3. **Look for the opportunity in every situation.** There is usually a "silver lining" if we will just look beyond the surface. In difficult situations, find the good that God is able to bring about as you trust Him and ask Him for the strength to overcome.

4. **When you start your day, ask God to open your eyes to His goodness** all around you. Every time you see God's goodness throughout the day – even in the smallest of things – thank Him!

PRAYER FOR EYES THAT SEE POTENTIAL

Father, open my eyes to see my full potential in Jesus. Destroy in me all mindsets that do not line up with Your truth concerning my life. May I be all that You have purposed for me to be. Allow me also, to see the potential that You have placed in others, so that I might affirm them according to Your vision and truth. Allow me to behold Your greatness. Amen.

CHAPTER 4

EYES THAT SEE THE KINGDOM

It is vital in this hour for believers to *see* with a Kingdom, or throne-room perspective. A Kingdom is a place where a king has rule. Jesus is the King of all kings, and His authority is over all other dominions and Kingdoms. We have the privilege of being seated in heavenly places with Him (Ephesians 2:6). When life and its struggles are viewed from this glorious position, it makes daily challenges look easy to overcome. Colossians 3:1-2 teaches us to *"seek those things with are above, where Christ is, sitting at the right hand of God. Set your mind on things above, not on things on the earth."* David said in Psalm 123:1, *"Unto You I lift up my eyes, O You who dwell in the heavens."* We are to focus on the King and His rule.

The Kingdom realm is full of blessings and realities for believers to behold. In God's Kingdom, we find heaven itself, His throne room, His angels, and all the spiritual blessings in the heavenly places in Christ. There are so many things for our spiritual vision to feast on.

GOD WANTS TO OPEN YOUR SPIRITUAL VISION

In the Bible, we find numerous accounts of God's people seeing into the spiritual realm. Isaiah saw the Lord in His throne room with the fiery seraphim proclaiming His holiness and glory while the smoke from the altar filled the temple (Isaiah 6). John, in the book of Revelation, records heavenly and divine encounters in the glory realm. Paul visited the third heaven.

Prophets like Daniel and Ezekiel went into the visions of God. Believers all throughout the Scriptures experienced angelic visitations. In 2 Kings 6:17, we discover Elisha praying that the *eyes* of his servant would be opened to *see* the angelic host that surrounded them in the ream of the spirit. They were in a very difficult situation at the time, but Elisha saw the victory because he had eyes to see into the Kingdom realm. He had assurance as a result of what he was able to see. His servant was also able to feel secure as a result of having his eyes opened through Elisha's prayer.

We find that many believers today are experiencing the opening of their spiritual eyes. They are beholding the glory, authority, and majesty of the Lord and His Kingdom.

The opening of spiritual vision is for all believers. We are especially finding that children are seeing into the realm of the spirit. You can, too. Jesus wants you to *see* clearly.

PREPARATION TO SEE THE KINGDOM

The following are some helpful, practical tips that will prepare you to see the Kingdom:

1. Begin to pray each day that the Father would "give to you a spirit of wisdom and of revelation in the knowledge of Him," and that "the eyes of your heart may be enlightened" (Ephesians 1:17-18).

2. Spend time meditating on passages in Scripture that give us a picture of God's eternal Kingdom, like Revelation 1:12-16; also chapter 4, Ezekiel 1, Daniel 7:9-14, and Isaiah 6:1-7.

3. As you read the Gospels (Matthew, Mark, Luke, and John), highlight in your Bible the word *Kingdom*. Notice how often Jesus talked about His Kingdom and the parables He shared to tell us what His Kingdom looks like.

4. Consider any hindrance that is clouding your vision and keeping you from fixing your eyes upon Jesus (meditate on Hebrews 12:1-2). Guard what you take in through your senses because Jesus said, "The pure in heart will see God" (Matthew 5:8).

PRAYER FOR EYES THAT SEE THE KINGDOM

Father, open my eyes to see the rule of Jesus and the glory of Your Kingdom. May I see the reality of Your presence, the angels, and the awesome creatures that serve and worship You. May I see the brilliance of the heavenly places and see the reality of Your Kingdom power and grace. Amen

CHAPTER 5

EYES THAT SEE PROPHETICALLY

In Bible days, the prophets were sometimes called "seers." This is because they experienced visions, impressions, and dreams from the Lord. Through their prophetic eyes, they could often see God's plans for the future as well as His strategies for their day.

The Lord has given His Church today prophetic vision and ability. Jesus explained to His disciples that the Holy Spirit would minister to believers by showing us things to come (see John 16:13). The gifts of the Holy Spirit are for every born-again Christian, and this includes the gift of prophecy, the word of knowledge, and the discerning of spirits. These are "seeing gifts," and most prophets operate well in these endowments. This does not mean, however, that all believers are called to be prophets—this is a special appointment by God for some in the Body. We are all called to be prophetic, though, and we are called to "see." Jesus explained to His disciples that the Holy Spirit would come to believers and show us things to come (see John 16:13). The Body of Christ is called to *see* with prophetic eyes.

Often within Scripture, the prophetic ministry of Jesus Christ is represented by the eagle. The eagle is a unique bird and has particular characteristics that symbolically speak of the type of vision the Lord has given to us. The eagle has a double membrane over its eyes that enables it to look directly into the sun. It is the only bird that is able to do so.

A second feature of the eagle's visionary ability is that it is able to see long distances. An eagle will soar high in the heavens, gazing into the sun, and then look down to earth with enhanced perspective, able to see with great precision. This, of course, is helpful when it is on the hunt for food.

The Lord desires his people to be like eagles – to soar into heavenly heights, gazing into His Presence, and then looking at earthly circumstances through His perspective.

In Acts 2:17-19, Peter quotes the prophecy of Joel, revealing the Lord's promise to pour out His Spirit upon all people in the last days. God says that through this outpouring, dreams, visions, and prophetic unction will released. The Lord is granting fresh moves of His presence today. As a result, we will increase in our spiritual vision. Dreams, visions, prophetic revelation and insight into the heavenly realm will manifest in our lives as we draw near to Him.

PREPARATION TO SEE PROPHETICALLY

The following are some helpful, practical tips that will prepare you to see prophetically:

1. **Pursue some good Bible training on the subject.** The Bible is your instruction book, and you can mature in prophetic gifting if you exercise its teachings by faith. There are also many training tools (seminars, audio training, workbooks, and books) by credible ministers that can be great coaches for your growth.

2. **Ask the Lord to help you remember the dreams you have at night** (everyone dreams every night, but many people do not remember their dreams or disregard them). God wants to speak to you at night as you are resting so that you can see your life from His perspective during the day.

3. **Share with others the potential you see in them.** Do this often! Declare over them the truth of who God has created them to be. This can be something as simple as expressing your appreciation for a quality they consistently demonstrate.

4. **Take a bit more time to look at a situation from God's point of view.** Remember to look at it through the lens of the cross (God's loves the world and came to save it). Spending time in God's presence will help you to soar into heavenly heights like the eagle, gaze

upon Him, and then look at earthly circumstances through His perspective.

Prayer for Eyes That See Prophetically

Father, grant me eyes to see from Your perspective. Please anoint my eyes to see with prophetic precision and accuracy. Pour out Your Spirit upon me afresh, and grant me the ability to see visions, dreams, and revelation of Your glory, splendor, and divine purposes. May You allow me to see your heavenly radiance. Amen.

CHAPTER 6

DISTORTED VISION

In Christ we have been graced with the ability to see as He sees. The more we posture ourselves before Him in purity and expectation, the more we will see. However, we have an enemy who is out to steal, kill, and destroy, and who blinds eyes to the light of the gospel of the glory of Christ (John 10:10; 2 Corinthians 4:4). The following are insights from the Scripture that warn us concerning vision distortions.

DOUBLE VISION

Jesus said the following:

"The lamp of the body is the eye. If therefore your eye is good, your whole body will be full of light. But if your eye is bad, your whole body will be full of darkness. If therefore the light that is in you is darkness, how great is that darkness! No one can serve two masters; for either he will hate the one and love the other, or else he will be loyal to the one and despise the other. You cannot serve God and mammon" (Matthew 6:22-24).

This Scripture teaches that if your heart is divided, then your vision will be clouded. Many things can divide our heart, and this portion particularly indicates that if we focus on money (mammon), we will be divided in our loyalties. If however, we keep our affections singularly towards the Lord, our eye will be good and our entire being will be filled with light.

DEFILED VISION

"There is nothing that enters a man from outside which can defile him; but the things which come out of him, those are the things that defile a man" (Mark 7:15).

Jesus further explained this point when He addressed the scribes, Pharisees, and hypocrites in Matthew 23:25-28. There are many things that can defile our hearts and therefore cloud our perceptions.

The following are some things that can distort our vision:

UNCLEANNESS AND LUST

"I say to you that whoever looks at a woman to lust for her has already committed adultery with her in his heart. If your right eye causes you to sin, pluck it out and cast it from you" (Matthew 5:28-29).

Jesus used very strong language, but it proves to us that our vision needs to be protected from uncleanness and lust. These things can distort and disturb holy vision and insight.

The lamp of the body is the eye (Matthew 6:22; Luke 11:34); therefore, we should be very careful concerning what we expose our eyes to. Suggestive scenes are often shown on television commercials and programs, as well as in movie theaters, magazines, and newspapers. Should we be submitting our vision to such uncleanness? Could this type of exposure actually darken our clear, holy, Kingdom vision? Let's be careful what we allow ourselves to look at with our natural vision. That which enters in through the eye gate will influence the soul.

JUDGMENT, BITTERNESS, AND HATRED

"Judge not, that you be not judged. For with what judgment you judge, you will be judged: and with the measure you use, it will be measured back to you.

And why do you look at the speck in your brother's eye, but do not consider the plank in your own eye?... Hypocrite! First **remove the plank from your own eye**, and then you will see clearly to remove the speck from your brother's eye" (Matthew 7:1-5, *emphasis added*).

This passage teaches that if we enter into judgment of others, we will not see clearly. When we critically judge others for their faults, we are then unable to see the very thing that has clouded our vision. Jesus teaches us to examine our own hearts and remove the "plank" that distorts our perception. Then we will "see clearly."

1 John 2:9-11 says:

"He who says he is in the light, and hates his brother, is in darkness until now. He who loves his brother abides in the light, and there is no cause for stumbling in him. But he who hates his brother is in darkness and walks in darkness, and does not know where he is going, because **the darkness has blinded his eyes**" *(emphasis added).*

Here the Bible teaches us that hatred towards another will actually blind our vision so that we cannot see.

PRIDE

These six things the Lord hates, Yes, seven are an abomination to Him: A proud **look**...(Proverbs 6:16-17).

God resists the proud, but gives grace to the humble (James 4:6).

If we have pride in our hearts, our Kingdom perception will be hindered and we will not be able to see through God's perspective. Pride actually activates a resistance from the Lord towards us.

NARROW VISION

If we are locked into narrow vision, our Kingdom vision will be limited and hindered. The Lord is great and His abilities are beyond our comprehension. In the story of Jesus feeding the multitudes from Mark 6:34-44, we find that He had compassion on the multitudes and desired to feed them. He instructed His disciples to *"give them something to eat"* (verse 37). The disciples could not see beyond their natural circumstances because their vision was too narrow. They allowed their logic to give them insight rather than their faith. Jesus then performed the miracle of the loaves and fishes in order to feed the five thousand. At that point, the vision of the disciples was opened wider to see the power and ability of Jesus at work.

I love Ephesians 3:20. "Now unto Him who is able to do exceedingly abundantly above all we could ask or think, according to the power that works in us." This is so amazing! No matter what we can think of or imagine, it is still much too small in comparison to what Jesus is able to do. Let's broaden our perspective and vision. He is a big God!

Religious Vision

A religious mindset is always based on man's own ability to accomplish the call and works of God. Every false religion is based on man's efforts to please God. Christianity, on the other hand, is based on what Christ Himself has accomplished for us. On the cross, He completed all the requirements for man's redemption. We, as His followers, respond to His love by simply believing in what He has accomplished for us, and allow Him, by faith, to live his life through us.

Religious vision is always based on outward appearances, but God looks at the heart (1 Samuel 16:7). True Kingdom vision is received through walking in a personal relationship with the Lord, while the source of religious vision is the soul of man.

The beginning of religious vision is found in the Garden of Eden. As the serpent was tempting the woman to eat of the fruit of the knowledge of good and evil, he said, *"You will not surely die. For God knows that in the day you eat of it* **your eyes will be opened,** *and you will be like God, knowing good and evil"* (Genesis 3:4-5). In other words, the devil was saying, "Go ahead, turn to your own logic and figure this one out yourself. Even though God said, 'Thou shalt not,' He actually didn't mean it."

Adam and Eve fell into the deceptive trap and the eyes of their carnal vision opened at that time. This dimension of man's understanding that opposes and overrides the Word of God influences us to this very day.

Our wills must be yielded to His. Every false religion is founded in this rebellion—the eyes of man's understanding cannot see the purposes of God when they are leaning on the carnal nature of man for perception. We must learn to feast off the Tree of Life—Jesus. Then, and only then, will our eyes be opened to the truth.

False religions, the occult, and the New Age movement are full of seekers. Their vision has been distorted and deceived due to the error they have submitted themselves to. If we have ever engaged in the beliefs of false religions, the occult, or New Age practices, we need to renounce that involvement. In such cases, our spiritual vision has been opened up to a wrong spirit or doctrine. Jesus' blood cleanses us from this type of defilement, but we need to go to Him and receive this purification and freedom.

LACK OF AWAKENED VISION

Sometimes, we are hindered from seeing through our "God-vision" simply because we have not received the opening of our spiritual vision. The prophet Elisha saw into the spirit realm on a regular basis (2 Kings 6). His spiritual vision had been opened. His servant, however, had not been enlightened in the same way. Elisha simply prayed for the servant's vision to be opened. In the same way, you can pray (or have someone else pray for you) to have your vision opened.

REMOVE DISTORTION AND SEE CLEARLY

The following are some helpful, practical tips that will help remove distorted vision and prepare you to see clearly.

OPENING THE VISION

The apostle Paul prayed for the spiritual vision of the church at Ephesus to be opened. He prayed:

> ...that the God of our Lord Jesus Christ, the Father of glory, may give to you a spirit of wisdom and of revelation in the knowledge of Him. I pray that the *eyes of your heart* may be *enlightened,* so that you will know what is the hope of His calling, what are the riches of the glory of His inheritance in the saints ,and what is the surpassing greatness of His power toward us who believe (emphasis added).

In Revelation 3:18, the church at Laodicea was exhorted to *"anoint your eyes with eye salve, that you may see."*

We can all have our spiritual vision opened. The Lord says in Luke 11:9-10, *"Ask, and it will be given to you; seek, and you will find; knock, and it will be opened to you. For everyone who asks receives, and he who seeks finds, and to him who knocks it will be opened."* So ask and receive!

CLEANSING THE VISION

If you have identified any hindrances to the opening of your spiritual eyes in this chapter, then simply bring those issues before the Lord in true humility and repentance. Invite Him to forgive and cleanse you and He will (see 1 John 1:9). This act of faith closes off any "landing strip" for the enemy's oppression.

If you have been involved in any practices where your spiritual vision has been opened up to demonic forces or false visionary encounters through occult activity, you will need to renounce the practices. Demonic spirits that are attached to these practices will need to be served "eviction notices" by commanding them, in Jesus' name, to leave your life. Sometimes further deliverance ministry is needed, but usually this is a very simple act of faith. *"Greater is He who is in you than he who is in the world"* (1 John 4:4, NASB).

Receive this promise from the Scriptures:

He who walks righteously and speaks uprightly, He who despises the gain of Oppressions, Who gestures with his hands, refusing bribes, Who stops his ears *from hearing of bloodshed, And shuts his eyes from seeing evil: He will dwell on high; His place of defense will be the fortress of rocks; Bread will be given him, his water will be sure (Isaiah 33:15-16).*

CONSECRATE YOUR VISION

In Psalm 119:37, the psalmist prayed a prayer of consecration regarding his vision: *"Turn away my eyes from looking at worthless things, and revive me in Your way."* The psalmist received the insight that his personal revival was in direct relationship to that which his eyes looked upon.

In Psalm 101:3, David made a covenant with his eyes when he said, *"I will set nothing wicked before my eyes."*

Consecration means *to set apart* for His glory. After we set apart our eyes (both spiritual and natural) for God's purposes, we can pray, *"Open my eyes, that I may see wondrous things from Your law"* (Psalm 119:18).

One of the faculties of our vision is imagination. The imagination is a created organ by God that enables us to "see." You will never have any type of vision without the imagination being engaged. It is the organ that records vision or image. The Holy Spirit imparts God-visions or pictures into the imagination so that we might "see." In Ephesians 1:18, Paul prayed for the church, that the eyes of their understanding would be enlightened, or opened. The word *understanding* in that passage is also translated from the original Greek as "imagination." In order for your imagination to be used by the Holy Spirit, it needs to be sanctified, or set it apart for God's purposes.

One of the ways to sanctify our imagination is to submit it to the Word of God, by meditating daily on passages that "paint pictures" in our heart.

ANOINT YOUR EYES WITH EYE SALVE

In Revelation 3:18, the Lord counseled those in the church of Laodicea to anoint their eyes with eye salve so that they would see. I believe this is speaking of allowing the Holy Spirit to anoint our vision. In John 9:39 we find Jesus saying, *"For judgment I have come into the world, that those who do not see may see, and that those who see may be made blind."*

We have mentioned the incident in the Garden of Eden where the eyes of Adam and Eve's carnal nature were opened. This was a fatal experience and brought separation between mankind and God. Jesus is saying that He came to "blind those that see." In His mercy, He is closing the eyes of our carnal nature for us.

I believe this is what happened to Saul during his Damascus experience. We see the account of the Lord's apprehension of Saul in Acts 9. In verses 8 and 9, we find that Saul is left without sight for three days.

The Lord then spoke to Ananias, instructing him very specifically to lay hands on Saul that he might receive his sight and be filled with the Spirit (verses 11, 12, 17). When Ananias did this, *"Immediately there fell from his eyes something like scales, and he received his sight at once"* (verse 19). The Holy Spirit's anointing was like eye salve, causing Saul to be blinded to his carnal vision, but his Kingdom vision was opened. He could now see through God's perspective. He was now able to see into the realm of truth—into the realm of God's glory. As a result, Saul was transformed. He had a name change (to Paul) and became the renowned "Apostle of Grace."

Prior to Paul's "sight conversion," he saw through eyes of error—through eyes of his intellect and religious understanding. He was very zealous for God and for His Word but did not have true knowledge because he could not see it. As a result, he persecuted the truth tellers.

This very pattern has been repeated throughout revival history in the Church. When the Lord introduces a fresh revelation of His truth to His people, some rise up to persecute the move with religious zeal, being blinded to what the Lord is doing. Why? Because they cannot see.

We also can be set up for failure in discerning the true moving of the Spirit when we lean to our own intellect and understanding. Instead, we should spend time in His presence, laying down our own thoughts, waiting on Him to reveal the truth to us. It is the Holy Spirit who does this work in us.

In Isaiah 6, we find that during his experience in the throne room of God, Isaiah came under great conviction.

He said, *"Woe is me, for I am undone...for my eyes have seen the King, the LORD of hosts"* (verse 5). He saw Jesus, the King, the Lord of hosts, in this holy encounter. Isaiah's eyes were opened to behold the revelation of Christ. He was purged with the fire of consecration in the presence of the Lord. Then he heard the voice of the Lord commissioning him, saying:

"Go, and tell this people: 'Keep on hearing, but do not understand; Keep on seeing but do not perceive.' Make the heart of this people dull and their ears heavy, and *shut their eyes; Lest they* **see with their eyes,** *and hear with their ears, and understand with their heart, and return and be healed"* (verses 9-10, emphasis added).

This portion of Scripture troubled me until I realized that it was a judgment from God based on His mercy. He was commissioning the prophet to pronounce a warning concerning the carnal nature and vision of man. When man is blinded to his carnal vision and understanding, then he will be motivated to cry out for the opening of true vision—beholding Jesus.

In Luke 4:18, we find Jesus reading out of the book of Isaiah, quoting, *"He has anointed Me...To proclaim liberty to the captives and* **recovery of sight to the blind**" (emphasis added).

By faith, we can approach the throne of grace with boldness to obtain mercy and to find grace to help in our time of need (see Hebrews 4:16). As we ask the Lord to blind our carnal vision and to open our Kingdom vision, He will be faithful to His word to perform it—and then we will *"see the King in His beauty"* (Isaiah 33:17).

Blind Bartimaeus was a beggar in Jesus' day who had a desperate desire to see. When he learned that Jesus was in town, he began to cry out in a loud voice, *"Jesus, son of David, have mercy on me!"* (Mark 10:47). He was so focused on his desire that when Jesus' followers tried to silence him, he refused. He knew that he was blind, and he knew that he wanted to see. Jesus, impressed with his persistence, called him to Himself and asked, *"What do you want me to do for you?"* (verse 51). Upon hearing his request, Jesus said, *"Go your way; your faith has made you well"* (verse 52). Bartimaeus immediately received his sight and followed Jesus, never returning to his old lifestyle.

If we identify our blindness and in desperation ask for sight, we will not be refused the answer to our request. The one remarkable characteristic of Bartimaeus was his persistent faith. Jesus desires us to have strong faith too so that we can receive His promises. We can receive increased spiritual vision, by faith. In Mark 11:24, Jesus said to His disciples, *"Whatever things you ask when you pray, believe that you receive them, and you will have them."* Faith is the connector to all the covenant promises—including eyes that see.

POSTURE YOURSELF TO SEE CLEARLY

How we posture ourselves toward the Lord is very important. If we seek Him, we will find Him. If we look, we will see. It is vital that we position ourselves to spend time in His presence while laying down our own agendas, our soulish mindsets, and our preconceived ideas. As we do so, we will see the glory of His being and His Kingdom revealed to our hearts. We will truly have *eyes that see*.

In John 17:24, Jesus prayed to His Father concerning us, "*Father, I desire that they also whom You gave Me may be with Me where I am*, **that they may behold My glory which You have given Me**" (emphasis added).

So come, beloved child of God. Come into His presence. His hand is extended to you. His heart is warm towards you. Come; yield; receive. You have been given eyes that see. Come into His presence and...see Jesus.

CHAPTER 7

WAYS TO SEE

The following are some of the ways that God helps us to see.

IMPRESSIONS IN THE IMAGINATION

The faint impressions in the mind and imagination are the most common ways God reveals vision to His people. Often believers do not feel this is a significant vision and that it is a lower level than perhaps an open vision. This is not true. There are no lower or higher levels of types of vision. They are simply different ways that God uses to reveal His will and purpose. Each way is precious if God is the source.

Most seasoned and credible prophets will confirm that the most predominant ways that God speaks to them is through the still small God-thoughts in the mind and the faint impressions in the imagination.

The main thing is to discern the source. Sometimes the impressions in our imagination are sourced in our natural or carnal thinking. I returned to my hotel room after ministering one night and slipped into bed to get a good night sleep. As I was settling I received the thought, "I would love some chocolate chip cookies." Not only was I thinking about those cookies, I could see the impression of them in my mind's eye. In fact, I could practically taste them. Now that vision was obviously not initiated or inspired by God! It came from my natural man. We learn to discern.

Some impressions come from the devil. A young man came to me asking for prayer. He was constantly vexed and tormented with graphic, perverted, sexual images in his mind. It was obvious that those images were not from God. He had submitted his "eye-gate" to pornography and the enemy had a foothold on his mind and imagination. He renounced the pornography, we ministered deliverance, and he received great freedom after prayer. Following the ministry he had to watch over his heart. If a tempting image came into his imagination, he resisted it and commanded it to go in Jesus' name. The source of those images was the devil.

Images in the imagination usually have some symbolic qualities and require interpretation from the Lord. After identifying a vision from God make inquiry of Him regarding the interpretation. Write down the vision or draw it. Ponder it. Ask God for insights and journal those insights.

Once you have a vision you can revisit it. It is recorded in your memory bank. Sometimes I will ponder a vision for months. I will deliberately reflect on it more and ask the Lord for further insight. During those times I often see more detail and the image gets brighter and more defined.

Ask the Holy Spirit to quicken Scriptures to you that not only confirm the vision, but also strengthen and enlarge the revelation the Lord is giving you through it.

OPEN VISIONS AND TRANCES

An open vision is seen through the natural eye. It is just like you see in the natural but it is spiritual. The prophets Isaiah, Jeremiah, Ezekiel, Daniel, Amos, and Zechariah all had open visions that are detailed in their respective books in the Old Testament. Stephen had an open vision of heaven and saw the glory of God and Jesus standing beside the Father while he was being stoned to death (see Acts 7:55-56). The apostle Paul had a vision of a man from Macedonia pleading with him to come to Macedonia to help them. They immediately left for Macedonia concluding that God was directing them to preach there (see Acts 16:9-10). The first time I saw an angel it was through an open vision.

Trances are similar to visions but they involve living in the dimension of what you see. When you are in a trance, you are inside the vision. The apostle Peter had a trance that completely shifted his perspective. A devout Jew, Peter probably had some very strong feelings about Gentiles, their role in the Kingdom of God and ability to enter into the fullness of Christ. God used a trance to change not only *his* thinking and approach to the Gentiles, but also that of the growing Church (see Acts 10).

Open visions and trances are not as common as impressions in the imagination but they are ways God speaks to His people at times.

DREAMS AND DAYDREAMS

Not all dreams or visions are sourced in God. The source always needs to be discerned. God can and does, however, reveal His will to His children in both night and day dreams.

He often chooses to speak through dreams because He can speak to our hearts while we are still and resting. Dreams also create a valuable journey of exploration for us. Most dreams are symbolic in nature and need interpretation. Following a God-inspired dream, you are invited to draw close to Him to inquire more of its meaning. All believers can interpret dreams because the interpretations belong to God and He has freely given us all things (see Genesis 40:8 and Romans 8:32).

Daniel 2 tells of when the ruler of Babylon, King Nebuchadnezzar, had a disturbing dream. When he awoke in the morning, he called his magicians, astrologers, sorcerers, and Chaldeans. They all said, "Tell us the dream and we'll give you its interpretation." But Nebuchadnezzar required them to tell him not only the interpretation, but also the dream itself! Because they couldn't do this, Nebuchadnezzar gave the order to destroy all the wise men of Babylon. But Daniel sought God and received the dream and accurate interpretation from the Lord in a night vision or dream. Daniel 2:19-23 says:

> So Daniel blessed the God of heaven. Daniel answered and said: "Blessed be the name of God forever and ever, for wisdom and might are His. And He changes the times and the seasons; He removes kings and raises up kings; He gives wisdom to the wise And knowledge to those who have understanding. He reveals deep and secret things; He knows what is in the darkness, and light dwells with Him. I thank You and praise You, O God of my fathers; You have given me wisdom and might, and have now made known to me what we asked of You, for You have made known to us the king's demand."

Daydreams are also a way that God speaks. I received my call to preach through a daydream years ago. I was in a women's conference as a new believer. The speaker stepped into the pulpit and began to preach. It was so powerful. I was hanging on every word and was completely focused. Suddenly, I realized I had drifted off into a daydream. In this daydream, I was preaching in the pulpit instead of her. I felt so guilty and wondered how I had become so delusional and proud. I quietly asked God to forgive me and resumed my focus on the message. I drifted off a second time and once again was alarmed at the realization. I repented and resumed focus the second time. It then happened a third time. I was undone. How could this have happened? I felt so guilty and after the meeting returned to my room and cried before the Lord asking Him to deliver me from pride and arrogance.

A few years later I received an invitation to share a testimony in the same room where this incident occurred. I had completely forgotten about the daydream and accepted the invitation. When it came time to preach and as I stepped into the pulpit (the same one as years before), the voice of the Lord spoke into my mind, "This day that daydream is fulfilled in your midst." I realized at that moment that the daydream had actually been the Lord revealing my call to preach. I have had many daydreams since that time that were God inspired.

CULTIVATING THE SEER ANOINTING

In the Old Testament, prophets that had visions were called seers. Their visions were sovereignly imparted to them by God. Many of their visions are recorded in the Scriptures for us to read and ponder. Prophets such as Ezekiel and Daniel were rich in visionary encounters and were gifted with the seer anointing. In the New Testament we find John living in the seer dimension as he described his encounters in heaven in the book of Revelation. Peter also saw a vision and was engaged in a God-inspired trance.

In Christ, all the law and the prophets are fulfilled. That means that Christ in you is the fulfillment of everything, and He is the Perfect Seer. Through Christ, you have access to the seer anointing.

Some believe that gifts cannot be cultivated and are always sovereign. I personally do not agree with this. For example, I know an individual who through the sovereignty of God learned to play the keyboard without one lesson. They literally sat down and began to play. God inspired and empowered them through supernatural grace and enablement. I also know individuals who are extremely gifted and anointed and learned through music lessons, practice, and more practice. They submitted themselves to years of training in order to carry the weight of glory they release in their ministries. Both ways are blessed of God.

I do not know of anyone who would oppose the idea of an individual submitting to training and practicing music in order to get seasoned and matured in the anointing to lead worship. Yet, there seems to be many who oppose the idea of training and practice in other aspects of the anointing such as the seer dimension.

You can mature in your ability to see. For example, the seer anointing can be cultivated and activated by meditating on the visions recorded in the Scripture. For example, read the vision of John in Revelation 1 of Jesus in the midst of the lampstands. Submit your imagination to the vision penned in Scripture and invite the Holy Spirit to reveal the vision to your own heart. Ponder the vision. Imagine each verse and concept while submitting to the Holy Spirit and the Word of God. By doing this, you are submitting yourself to the seer anointing of God that originally inspired the vision.

Another thing that is helpful to awaken the seer anointing is to draw the vision you are meditating on and then fill it in with color and detail. Invite the Holy Spirit to reveal His heart and ways through the exercise.

After meditating on the visions in Scripture, wait on the Lord and invite Him to reveal vision to you. No matter how the visions come, celebrate each one. Write them down, draw them, and then make inquiry of the Lord concerning them. This practice of working through the vision will cultivate the seer anointing in you.

A PRAYER FOR YOU

Jesus said, *"Most assuredly, I say to you, the Son can do nothing of Himself, but what He sees the Father do; for whatever He does, the Son also does in like manner"* (John 5:29). You are called to be just like Jesus. You have been given eyes to see, and see you will.

Father, in Jesus' name I pray for my friends that they might see as You see. Open their vision to behold the most amazing glimpses of Your glory and Kingdom. Grant unto them revelations, visions, impressions, and dreams. Fulfill their deepest desire to see. May they truly have their Father's eyes. Amen.

Now beloved... look and see.

PERSONAL NOTES

PERSONAL NOTES

PATRICIA KING

Patricia is president of both Extreme Prophetic and Christian Services Association. She has been a pioneering voice in ministry, with over 30 years of background as a Christian minister in conference speaking, prophetic service, church leadership, and television and radio appearances. Patricia has written numerous books, produced many CDs and DVDs, hosts Extreme Prophetic TV, and is the CEO of a popular online media network – XPmedia.com. Patricia's reputation in the Christian community is world-renowned.

Christian Services Association (CSA) was founded in Canada in 1973 and in the USA in 1984. It is the parent ministry of Extreme Prophetic, a 501(c)(3) founded in 2004 in Arizona. CSA/Extreme Prophetic is located in Maricopa, AZ and Kelowna, B.C. Patricia King and numerous team members equip the body of Christ in the gifts of the Spirit, prophetic ministry, intercession, and evangelism. CSA/Extreme Prophetic is called to spreading the gospel through media.

AUTHOR CONTACT INFORMATION

Extreme Prophetic/CSA
U.S. Ministry Center
P.O. Box 1017
Maricopa, AZ 85139

XP Canada Ministry Center
3054 Springfield Road
Kelowna, B.C V1X 1A5
CANADA

Telephone: 1-250-765-9286
E-Mail: info@XPmedia.com

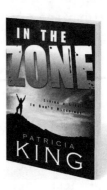

Keys to Living in the Glory Realm!

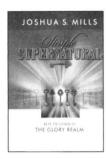

Simple Supernatural. Every believer in Christ is a supernatural being with a supernatural purpose, called to walk in the supernatural ways of heaven while demonstrating God's supernatural Kingdom here on earth!

Joshua Mills shares exciting personal testimonies, biblical keys, and practical guidelines that will launch you into a supernatural lifestyle. Learn how to live in the Glory Realm, win souls supernaturally, manifest God's Word and heal the sick, and more!

Marriage at Its Best!

Supernatural Marriage. Dan Wilson. The key to supernatural marriage is Spirit led intimacy, which makes it possible to successfully enter the extreme and satisfying intimacy of marriage. Man, woman, and God are brought together to create an entity that Satan has no reliable way to attack, no useful battle plan to defeat, and no effective weapon to destroy. A timely and needed message for all married couples!